Original title:
Nurturing Your Love

Copyright © 2024 Swan Charm
All rights reserved.

Author: Paula Raudsepp
ISBN HARDBACK: 978-9916-89-046-2
ISBN PAPERBACK: 978-9916-89-047-9
ISBN EBOOK: 978-9916-89-048-6

Together in the Moment

In the quiet morn, we rise,
Sunlight dances in our eyes.
Hand in hand, hearts intertwined,
In this moment, peace we find.

Laughter echoes in the air,
Joyful whispers without a care.
Every second feels so right,
Together, we embrace the light.

Through the trials, we stand tall,
Supporting each other through it all.
In each heartbeat, we believe,
Together we can always achieve.

As the stars adorn the night,
We share our dreams, fueling the light.
In the silence, love's sweet song,
Together is where we belong.

With every breath, we draw nearer,
The world fades, our hearts are clearer.
Together, in this fleeting time,
We create a rhythm, a perfect rhyme.

Nurtured by Time

In the garden, seeds are sown,
With caring hands, love has grown.
Each petal soft, each leaf a sign,
Nurtured gently, a bond divine.

In the stillness of the night,
Time whispers softly, a guiding light.
Every moment, cherished, adored,
Through every challenge, we're restored.

As seasons change and years unfold,
Our story deepens, rich and bold.
In the arms of time, we thrive,
Nurtured by love, we come alive.

With roots that dig and branches wide,
We stand together, side by side.
Through storms and sunshine, we prevail,
Nurtured by time, we will not fail.

In memories, we find our grace,
Time's gentle touch leaves a trace.
With every heartbeat, we ascend,
Nurtured together, till the end.

Ties That Bind

In the weave of days we share,
Threads of laughter fill the air.
Moments stitched, a colorful blend,
Forever tied, we won't descend.

Through storms and trials, hand in hand,
Hearts compose a loyal band.
With each heartbeat, love defined,
In every clash, our souls aligned.

Days grow long, yet we remain,
In every joy, in all the pain.
Through years that pass, our roots run deep,
In the bonds we've made, we find our keep.

Sweet Echoes of Care

In whispers soft, the night reveals,
The warmth of love, the heart appeals.
Gentle notes in twilight's glow,
In caring hearts, our kindness flows.

A helping hand, a knowing smile,
Compassion shared, it's worth the while.
Through every trial, steadfast we stand,
In sweet echoes, life's hand in hand.

Each gesture small, yet filled with grace,
In simple acts, we find our place.
With every word, a bond we share,
In gentle echoes, proof of care.

The Hearth of Togetherness

A fire burns, its flicker bright,
In the center, warmth ignites.
Gathered close, our stories flow,
In every glance, the love we show.

Laughter dances, shadows play,
In this haven, come what may.
Tomorrow's dreams weave through the night,
In the hearth, our spirits light.

Families gather, friends unite,
In this space, the world feels right.
With every season, new tales grow,
In the heart's embrace, together we glow.

Embracing Quiet Moments

In stillness found, the world takes pause,
In gentle whispers, nature draws.
A quiet breath, the stars align,
In these moments, hearts entwine.

Time slows down, worries fade,
In soft embrace, our thoughts cascade.
With every sigh, we learn to hear,
The quiet joys that bring us near.

In tranquil spaces, love resides,
Through silent paths, true peace abides.
Moments cherished, soft and bright,
In quietude, our souls take flight.

Threads of Tenderness

In whispers soft as morning light,
We weave our dreams, hopes taking flight.
With gentle hands, we stitch each seam,
Creating warmth, a shared soft dream.

Through every laugh and tender sigh,
Connections bloom, like stars in sky.
In every glance, a story told,
In threads of love, our hearts unfold.

A tapestry of days gone by,
In memories spun, we learn to fly.
With every moment, we grow strong,
In this sweet dance, where we belong.

Together we face the storms that rise,
Holding each other beneath dark skies.
In harmony, our spirits blend,
In threads of tenderness, we mend.

As seasons change, our colors bright,
With every heartbeat, we take flight.
In the fabric of our sweet embrace,
We find our home, our sacred space.

The Art of Caring

In simple acts, the heart takes flight,
A hand to hold, a smile so bright.
With gentle words, we lift the veil,
In caring moments, love prevails.

A listening ear in times of need,
Each thoughtful gesture plants a seed.
In quiet ways, we show we care,
A sacred bond, so sweet and rare.

Through storms of life, we stand as one,
In every challenge, we have won.
With open hearts and tender grace,
We paint the world with warm embrace.

The art of caring, soft and true,
In every action, love shines through.
In shared laughter, in shared tears,
We build a bridge that calms our fears.

Together we navigate the night,
With love as anchor, shining bright.
In every heartbeat, a lasting song,
In the art of caring, we belong.

Serene Moments Between Us

In quiet corners, time stands still,
Serene moments gently fill.
With tranquil hearts, we share our dreams,
In soft whispers, the silence gleams.

Beneath the stars, our laughter flows,
In gentle breezes, our love grows.
Each fleeting glance, a world apart,
In tender stillness, we find heart.

In golden sunsets, hand in hand,
Together we walk, love's soft strand.
In peaceful sways, the world we know,
In serene moments, our spirits glow.

Through every trial, we find our peace,
In heartbeats shared, our worries cease.
In the quiet spaces, we are free,
In serene moments, just you and me.

With every sunset, our story blooms,
In gentle waves, love softly looms.
Between our breaths, the magic lies,
In serene moments, love never dies.

A Symphony of Hearts

In harmony, our souls align,
A symphony of hearts divine.
With every note, a story swells,
In love's embrace, where music dwells.

With gentle rhythms, we take flight,
In melodies that dance with light.
Each whispered dream, a lilting string,
In cadence sweet, our spirits sing.

The world around us fades away,
In symphonies, we'll always stay.
Through every trial, we play our part,
Each beat and measure, a work of art.

In laughter and tears, a perfect score,
Together we find what hearts adore.
In every chord, our spirits play,
In a symphony that guides our way.

So let us dance to love's soft tune,
Under the stars, beneath the moon.
In every heartbeat, timeless charts,
Writing a song of symphonic hearts.

Crafting Our Masterpiece

With every brushstroke bold,
We paint our dreams in gold.
Together hands entwined,
Creating worlds aligned.

Every color tells a tale,
Of journeys where we sail.
In laughter we ignite,
This canvas of delight.

Through shadows, light will dance,
In harmony, we prance.
With passion, we will mold,
A story to be told.

Each layer that we lay,
Turns night into the day.
In flaws, we find our grace,
Our masterpiece, our space.

In moments we define,
A love, a sip of wine.
Each stroke, a bond so deep,
Awake or lost in sleep.

Garden of Mutual Growth

In soil rich and pure,
Our roots begin to stir.
With care, we cultivate,
A bond that won't abate.

Beneath the sun's warm light,
We flourish day and night.
In every bloom we see,
The strength in you and me.

The rain may come to fall,
Yet we will stand up tall.
In storms, we grow more strong,
Together, where we belong.

With petals soft and bright,
We share our pure delight.
In this garden we tend,
Love's harvest never ends.

So come, let's plant a seed,
In trust, we plant the need.
With every season's turn,
In our hearts, we will learn.

Shared Smiles in Twilight

As the sun bids goodbye,
We watch the colors fly.
With silhouettes in grace,
We share a quiet space.

In whispers soft and low,
Our laughter starts to flow.
The twilight paints the sky,
With dreams that lift us high.

Where shadows softly blend,
Our hearts begin to mend.
In this moment, so sweet,
Together, we find peace.

With fingers intertwined,
A treasure, purely mine.
In stillness, time will freeze,
Shared smiles, a gentle breeze.

Embracing fleeting light,
Through every starry night.
In twilight, love's embrace,
We find our perfect place.

Hearts Like a Safe Haven

In the silence we find,
A refuge for the mind.
With warmth, we build a space,
Where hearts can interlace.

Through trials, we will stand,
Together, hand in hand.
In storms that seem to rage,
Our love will turn the page.

With laughter like a song,
In this place we belong.
Safe harbor from life's strife,
Together, we find life.

In whispers of the heart,
A promise from the start.
With kindness, we will weave,
A tapestry to believe.

In this haven we share,
Each burden laid so bare.
With every dawn anew,
Our hearts, forever true.

Sculpting Our Togetherness

With hands that shape our dreams,
We mold the clay of hope.
Each gentle touch redeems,
In unity, we cope.

Through laughter and through tears,
We build a strong embrace.
In moments, love appears,
A bond time can't erase.

With every flaw, we're whole,
Each scar tells our dear tale.
Together, we console,
In storms, we will not pale.

Our hearts a sculptor's art,
Connected by our grace.
In rhythm, never part,
In time's enduring race.

As seasons flow like streams,
We carve our lives anew.
In all our shared dreams,
Together, we break through.

Hearts in Harmony

Two hearts beat as one tonight,
In sync with every breath.
Together, we find light,
In love, defying death.

With every note we play,
A symphony unfolds.
In joy or pain, we stay,
Embracing what life holds.

Our laughter fills the air,
In whispers, secrets shared.
In silence, we both care,
In trust, we are prepared.

As time unwinds the thread,
We weave a rich design.
In colors brightly spread,
Our fates so intertwined.

In harmony, we grow,
A dance beneath the stars.
With every high and low,
Our love heals every scar.

The Warmth We Weave

In twilight's gentle glow,
We spin our threads of gold.
With every story told,
A blanket of love grows.

As seasons start to change,
We gather in our strength.
In hands, our hearts exchange,
Filling in every length.

Through storms and sunny days,
We stitch our dreams right tight.
In laughter's joyful plays,
We find our shared delight.

With symbols we create,
A tapestry of hope.
Together, we translate,
The love that helps us cope.

In warmth, we find our way,
Each fiber holds our care.
In every night and day,
We're woven strong and rare.

Together Through Seasons

As spring returns with bloom,
We walk along the path.
In nature's sweet perfume,
We cherish every laugh.

With summer's warm embrace,
We dance beneath the sun.
In love, we find our place,
Together, we're as one.

As autumn leaves us gold,
We hold each other near.
In stories shared and told,
We banish doubt and fear.

Through winter's coldest night,
We snuggle side by side.
In each other's warm light,
Our hearts take loving pride.

In every passing phase,
We grow and learn anew.
Together, come what may,
Our bond is tried and true.

Cradled in Connection

In the hush of soft whispers,
Hearts entwined like vines,
Every glance, a promise,
Time gently unwinds.

Under the moon's tender glow,
Laughter dances in the air,
With every shared secret,
Love's a fragrant prayer.

Hands clasped in warm silence,
Two souls beat as one,
In the embrace of knowing,
Life's journey's just begun.

Through storms and the shadows,
Together we face the night,
With you, my heart's anchor,
In love's steady light.

As we weave our stories,
In threads of golden hue,
Cradled in connection,
My heart belongs to you.

Love's Gentle Haven

Nestled in your warmth,
A harbor profound and deep,
Each whisper a soft promise,
In your arms, I safely sleep.

The world fades to a whisper,
As your heartbeat sings,
In love's gentle haven,
I find my cherished wings.

Every moment we gather,
Like pearls upon a string,
In laughter, in silence,
Together, we take wing.

Seasons may change swiftly,
Through trials we will flow,
With love as our compass,
In faith, we shall grow.

A sanctuary in your gaze,
Where dreams and hopes reside,
Love's gentle haven,
Forever, side by side.

Caresses of Caring

In the quiet of the evening,
Soft touch of your hand,
Every caress like a whisper,
In warmth, calmly we stand.

With laughter echoing sweetly,
We dance through the days,
Tangled in all our moments,
A symphony of rays.

Through trials that may test us,
Your support is my shield,
In the garden of belonging,
Our love will never yield.

Each embrace tells a story,
In kindness, we find grace,
Caresses of caring,
In this sacred space.

With every promise we nurture,
Love blossoms like a flower,
In the caresses of caring,
We bloom with endless power.

Sewn with Sweetness

In threads of vibrant colors,
We stitch our lives with care,
Each moment an intention,
Wisdom woven rare.

With laughter as our needle,
And warmth to bind the seams,
Sewn with sweetness and solace,
In the fabric of our dreams.

Together we create magic,
In patterns bold and bright,
With every shared adventure,
We craft our own sunlight.

Through storms, we find our shelter,
In love's embrace so tight,
Sewn with sweetness and courage,
We conquer every night.

Every stitch holds a memory,
Each moment, pure and true,
Sewn with sweetness, our story,
Forever me and you.

Cherished Days and Nights

In the morning sun we rise,
With laughter dancing in our eyes.
Each moment holds a special grace,
A memory time cannot erase.

As stars ignite the evening sky,
With whispered dreams we softly sigh.
Together in the quiet glow,
Our hearts entwined, a gentle flow.

Seasons change, but we remain,
Through joy and sorrow, love's refrain.
In every hug, in every kiss,
We find the warmth of perfect bliss.

A tapestry of moments spun,
With every laugh, our hearts have won.
In cherished days, our story's told,
A treasure vast, more precious than gold.

So here we stand, hand in hand,
In life's great journey, we understand.
Each day, each night, a sweet embrace,
In cherished love, we find our place.

The Light We Share

Beneath the canopy of stars,
We find solace, even from afar.
Your laughter shines, a guiding light,
A beacon in the darkest night.

When shadows fall and doubts arise,
You'll be the spark that never dies.
In every glance, a promise made,
A bond so strong it won't ever fade.

With gentle words, you calm my fears,
A symphony that soothes the tears.
Together, we create a fire,
Fueling dreams, igniting desire.

In simple moments, joy unfolds,
A shared glance, a hand to hold.
The light between us, pure and bright,
Illuminates our endless flight.

So here's to us, to every sigh,
To whispered secrets, as we fly.
In this journey, forever we'll dare,
In love, in hope, the light we share.

Gentle Currents of Emotion

Like rivers winding through the land,
Our feelings flow, a delicate strand.
With every ripple, stories weave,
In silent whispers, we believe.

The touch of hands, a spark ignites,
Providing warmth on coldest nights.
In gentle waves, our hearts align,
A dance of souls, pure and divine.

Through laughter shared and tears we shed,
The currents guide where love has led.
In every heartbeat, trust is found,
A melody of softest sound.

As tides may rise and winds may change,
Our bond remains, though times feel strange.
For in the depths, we understand,
This ocean vast, a sacred land.

So let us sail on, side by side,
Through calm and storm, our hearts abide.
In gentle currents, we will stay,
Navigating love, come what may.

Rooted in Trust

In quiet moments, roots run deep,
Through whispers shared, our secrets keep.
A foundation strong, we've built with care,
In every glance, a life we share.

Through winds that shake and storms that rage,
Our trust endures, a sacred page.
With open hearts, we dare to grow,
Embracing all the seeds we sow.

In laughter bright and shadows cast,
Together, we've faced every blast.
Our branches stretch towards the sun,
In unity, two lives as one.

Through trials faced, we stand as two,
In every challenge, trust shines through.
A steady hand, a guiding heart,
From rooted love, we will not part.

So here we stand, strong and free,
Embracing all that's meant to be.
Rooted in trust, we will rise,
Against the storm, we'll touch the skies.

Love's Gentle Rain

In the quiet of the night,
Soft whispers fill the air,
Each drop a loving note,
Kissing hearts laid bare.

Amidst the darkened clouds,
Hope begins to grow,
With every tender raindrop,
A warm and gentle flow.

Through the windows of the soul,
Sunshine breaks the gray,
Love's gentle rain is falling,
Washing fears away.

Underneath the silver sky,
Hearts entwined like vines,
In the soft embrace of love,
Every moment shines.

As the storm begins to fade,
Rainbows start their dance,
In the aftermath of love,
We find our second chance.

Caring Hands and Heartstrings

Hands that cradle softly,
Painting warmth with a touch,
In the dance of life we find,
Caring means so much.

Fingers interlaced with hope,
Binding hearts as one,
Through the trials and laughter,
A journey just begun.

With every heartbeat echoing,
A song that never fades,
Together we build a refuge,
In love's warm serenades.

Heartstrings pull us closer,
In a melody so sweet,
Each note a promise given,
With a rhythm in our feet.

In the garden of affection,
We bloom like roses fair,
Caring hands, heartstrings tied,
Creating love's warm air.

In the Shade of Affection

Beneath the leafy canopy,
Where secrets softly blend,
In the shade of affection,
Love knows no end.

Moments shared in silence,
Whispers in the breeze,
Every look a promise,
Time itself we seize.

Gentle breezes carry dreams,
As shadows dance and play,
In this sacred space of heart,
We find our way.

Sunshine filters through the leaves,
Painting paths of light,
Guiding souls through laughter,
Holding love so tight.

In the shade of summer's grace,
Stories intertwine,
Embraced by nature's beauty,
Our hearts forever shine.

Love's Timeless Tapestry

Weaving threads of memories,
In colors bold and bright,
Each stitch a gentle heartbeat,
In the fabric of our light.

With every careful pattern,
Stories come alive,
In love's vast tapestry,
Together we will thrive.

Through valleys deep and mountains high,
Our tales begin to blend,
In the tapestry of time,
Love is the thread we send.

Moments stitched with laughter,
And tears that often flow,
In this rich collection,
Our hearts forever grow.

As the tapestry unfolds,
Each chapter shines anew,
In love's embrace we flourish,
Hand in hand, me and you.

Threads of Togetherness

In the quiet weave of night,
We gather threads of soft delight.
Each moment sewn with care,
Binding souls, a love laid bare.

Though the world may often stray,
In our hearts, we choose to stay.
With laughter stitched in every seam,
Together, we create a dream.

Through seasons change and ebbing flow,
Our bond remains a lovely glow.
Like a tapestry, we blend,
Threads of joy that never end.

In storms that rattle, winds that blow,
We shield the warmth of what we know.
A unity that will endure,
In threads of love, we find our cure.

And as we age, with silver hue,
We'll look back on the joys we knew.
Forever bound in this embrace,
Threads of togetherness in grace.

Heartbeats in Harmony

In the stillness of the dawn,
A rhythm beats, a gentle song.
With every pulse, I feel you near,
A melody we both hold dear.

Each heartbeat whispers soft and low,
A language only we both know.
In sync, our souls take flight,
Together dancing in the light.

With every thump, a story told,
Of love that's warm and never cold.
A harmony that fills the air,
In every breath, we find our prayer.

Through distant lands and time apart,
I feel your beat within my heart.
A serenade that never fades,
In each embrace, our serenades.

So let the world whirl madly round,
In us, the sweetest sound is found.
Our heartbeats sing a timeless tune,
In perfect harmony, beneath the moon.

Light of Kindred Spirits

In the glow of twilight's grace,
I find the warmth of your embrace.
With each laugh, the stars ignite,
Guiding us through the quiet night.

Together we chase the fading sun,
A journey shared by two as one.
With every step, our spirits soar,
Embracing love, always wanting more.

In whispers soft, our secrets shared,
A bond unbreakable, always cared.
With every flicker, every spark,
You light the path when it grows dark.

Through valleys deep and mountains high,
We journey forth, our heads held high.
The universe, a canvas bright,
Painted with our love's pure light.

And when the shadows close in tight,
I'll find you there, my guiding light.
Together we'll shine, forever true,
In the heart of all we do.

The Canvas of Us

With every brushstroke, colors blend,
A masterpiece that has no end.
On this canvas, we craft our dreams,
In vivid tones and flowing streams.

Each moment splashed with joy and pain,
A tapestry of sunshine and rain.
Through thick and thin, we paint with heart,
Creating art, never apart.

The hues that dance, the shades that sing,
In every corner, memories cling.
With laughter bright, and tears that fall,
We find the beauty in it all.

As layers build, our story grows,
In every line, our love bestows.
The canvas tells the tale so true,
Of how I cherish, love, and view.

And as we step back to see the view,
A life well-lived, with shades anew.
Together painted, side by side,
On this canvas, we abide.

Painting Our Tomorrow

With brushes bright, we start our dreams,
Colors blend in sunlit streams.
Each stroke a wish, each hue a song,
In this canvas, we all belong.

The future calls with voices clear,
A masterpiece, we hold so dear.
Together we will find our way,
In vibrant shades of every day.

With gentle hands, we craft our fate,
In every line, we celebrate.
Upon this canvas, hearts will meet,
Our painted path, a rhythm sweet.

With every color, truth unfolds,
A tapestry of stories told.
In every corner, hope will shine,
As we create a world divine.

So let us paint, with love and light,
A tomorrow full of pure delight.
With every vision, bold and free,
Together, just you wait and see.

Threads of Time

Weaving tales from days gone by,
Threads of time, they weave and tie.
Each moment's fabric, rich and bright,
In shadows, whispers take their flight.

The tapestry of life we share,
Intertwined with love and care.
With every stitch, a story spun,
In this we find the hearts of one.

Golden strands of joy and pain,
In every joy, in every rain.
So let the loom of life be strong,
With threads of right, and threads of wrong.

Through every decade, memories blend,
Past and future, they twist and bend.
In every layer, truths revealed,
The fabric of our lives unsealed.

As seasons change and ages flow,
The threads of time continue to grow.
With every weave, a life in view,
A bond of history, tried and true.

Embracing Every Season

In spring's sweet whisper, hope awakes,
Young blooms dance as the morning breaks.
With every petal, life ignites,
In every color, pure delights.

Summer brings its golden rays,
Longer days and laughter's blaze.
Joy in every sunlit kiss,
Nature's chorus, endless bliss.

Autumn's brush turns leaves to gold,
As stories from the trees are told.
The harvest moon, bright in the night,
Wraps us in warmth, a soft twilight.

With winter's chill, we gather near,
Fireside tales and love sincere.
In starlit skies, we find our peace,
A time for rest and sweet release.

Each season comes with lessons learned,
Through every turn, new passions burned.
So let us dance through every change,
In nature's arms, forever strange.

The Shelter of Understanding

In quiet moments, hearts align,
A refuge built, by design.
With open arms, we share our fears,
In this cocoon, we dry our tears.

Through storms that rage, we stand as one,
With every word, a battle won.
In empathy, we find our strength,
Building bridges at any length.

Each story told, a thread we weave,
In every truth, we can believe.
No judgment cast, just gentle light,
A guiding star through darkest night.

With kindness, we embrace the way,
In understanding, we choose to stay.
Together safe, we face the world,
With compassion's banner, unfurled.

In this sweet space, we come alive,
With love and hope, we learn to thrive.
In every heart, a home we find,
The shelter of our shared, kind mind.

Moments of Pure Connection

In silent glances, hearts collide,
A language spoken, none can hide.
The fleeting time, a precious thread,
In every beat, the words unsaid.

A smile reveals what's deep inside,
In laughter shared, the joys reside.
A gentle touch, a soft caress,
In simple clouds, our dreams express.

Beneath the stars, we find our place,
In every shadow, we leave a trace.
The moments shared, forever bind,
In pure connection, love aligned.

With whispered thoughts that intertwine,
In fleeting seconds, love's design.
Our paths converge, our spirits soar,
In finest threads, we weave once more.

Through time and space, our hearts will meet,
In every heartbeat, love's heartbeat.
The sacred bond that time can't sever,
In moments pure, we shine forever.

Warmth in the Embrace

A gentle hug, a quiet night,
In arms that hold, everything's right.
The warmth that melts the coldest fears,
In tender love, we dry our tears.

With every sigh, the world fades away,
In whispered dreams, we choose to stay.
The fire's glow, a soft delight,
In each embrace, we find our light.

The comfort found in soft skin's grace,
In every heartbeat, a sacred space.
Together we breathe, the world aligned,
In warmth divine, our hearts entwined.

When shadows loom and troubles rise,
In loving touch, our spirits fly.
The shelter here, in love's embrace,
In gentle warmth, we find our place.

The night is long, but we are near,
In woven souls, we banish fear.
With open hearts, we face the dawn,
In every hug, a love reborn.

Love's Guiding Light

In darkest times, your light will glow,
A beacon bright, through high and low.
The path we tread, with love so clear,
In every step, your heart is near.

Each whispered word, a spark ignites,
In tender moments, love's pure sights.
With eyes that shine, the dreams ignite,
In trust and hope, we take to flight.

Through storms that rage and winds that wail,
Together we shall always prevail.
With every doubt, a strength we find,
In love's embrace, we're intertwined.

Your laughter is a song I crave,
In every heart, your love's the wave.
With open arms, the future's bright,
In every moment, love's guiding light.

With promises made beneath the stars,
In every journey, no matter how far.
We walk together, hand in hand,
In love's great light, forever we'll stand.

The Bonding of Kindred Souls

In sacred spaces where hearts align,
Two spirits dance, a love divine.
With every glance, a story told,
In laughter shared, our hearts unfold.

Through trials faced and dreams we chase,
In whispered secrets, we find our place.
The bond we share, a force of fate,
In every moment, love's true state.

With every challenge, we stand tall,
In unity's strength, we conquer all.
The ties that bind, the roots run deep,
In loyalty's embrace, our dreams we keep.

In silent nights, our hearts converse,
In words unspoken, we both immerse.
The depth we share, no words explain,
In kindred souls, forever remain.

When paths may bend and time may stray,
In love's embrace, we find our way.
The journey's long, but side by side,
In kindred souls, forever abide.

Flourishing Affections

In the garden of dreams we grow,
Where sunlight dances, hearts aglow.
Petals whisper secrets of grace,
In each embrace, time finds its place.

Tender glances, soft and warm,
Through life's seasons, a gentle charm.
With every laugh, a bond so bright,
Together we flourish, love's pure light.

Nurtured roots in fertile ground,
In quiet moments, joy is found.
With every heartbeat, love ignites,
A symphony of shared delights.

Through storms of doubt and skies of gray,
Our flourishing spirit lights the way.
Hand in hand, we face each test,
In love's embrace, we are truly blessed.

As blossoms bloom, together we'll stand,
In a world of wonders, hand in hand.
For in this dance of hearts entwined,
Flourishing affections, forever aligned.

Hand in Hand

Walking paths where shadows play,
With every step, we find our way.
Side by side, through thick and thin,
In love's embrace, new dreams begin.

With laughter shared in whispered tones,
Together we build a life of homes.
Through trials faced and joys we've planned,
In every moment, hand in hand.

Veils of night may cloak our sight,
But with you, love brings the light.
Through winding roads that twist and bend,
On this journey, you are my friend.

When autumn leaves fall, we will glide,
In the warmth of each other, we confide.
Through seasons changing, we will stand,
In every heartbeat, hand in hand.

For all our years, both young and old,
Together we write stories untold.
In every heartbeat, every strand,
We weave our love, hand in hand.

Cherished Footprints

In the sands of time we leave our mark,
Each step we take ignites a spark.
Footprints cherished, memories near,
With every moment, love sincere.

Through fields of laughter, we will roam,
In every heartbeat, you've made me home.
With gentle whispers, the winds will tell,
Of cherished footprints where we fell.

Paths we've walked and dreams we've dared,
In the tapestry of life, we're paired.
With every joy and tear that's shed,
Our cherished footprints, never misled.

In sunlit mornings and moonlit nights,
In shared glances, our hearts take flight.
With every journey hand in hand,
Our cherished footprints part of the land.

As seasons change and moments flee,
Each footprint tells our story, you and me.
In the album of time, forever stay,
Cherished footprints that light our way.

A Chorus of Heartstrings

In the silence where whispers sing,
Our love creates a vibrant ring.
Each heartbeat echoes, sweet and bright,
A chorus of heartstrings in the night.

With melodies of joy, we play,
Harmonizing hopes in a playful sway.
Together we dance, a timeless art,
A symphony composed from the heart.

Through every trial, every tear,
The music of us draws ever near.
In every note, our souls entwined,
A chorus of heartstrings, truly aligned.

As the stars emerge in the sky,
In their glow, our dreams will fly.
A melody lasting through the years,
Our chorus of heartstrings calms all fears.

For the songs we sing, both soft and grand,
Will linger forever, love's gentle band.
In the silence where whispers cling,
We find our strength, a chorus, we bring.

Whispers of Affection

In the quiet night we share,
Words unspoken fill the air.
Each soft glance, a gentle call,
Whispers of affection, binding all.

Stars above, they softly gleam,
We dance together, lost in dream.
With every heartbeat, love takes flight,
Whispers echo in the night.

Your laughter sparkles like the dew,
In every moment, I find you.
Beneath the moon's soft, silver light,
We weave our dreams, hearts intertwined.

Time stands still as shadows play,
In your embrace, I long to stay.
With every sigh, I feel the spark,
Whispers glow within the dark.

Let our secrets softly blend,
In this love that has no end.
Forever cherished, hearts align,
Whispers of affection, so divine.

Blossoms in the Heart

Petals falling, soft and pure,
In my heart, your love's the cure.
Each moment shared, a fragrant bloom,
Blossoms thrive within our room.

Sunlight spills through leafy trees,
Bringing warmth upon the breeze.
With every laugh, a flower grows,
Blossoms in the heart bestows.

Tender touch, like morning light,
Ignites the day, dispels the night.
Together, we create a new,
Blossoms blooming, me and you.

In every season, love's embrace,
Paints the world in vibrant grace.
With every heartbeat, colors start,
Blossoms flourish in the heart.

So let us tend this garden fair,
With gentle hands and loving care.
Each cherished moment, like fine art,
Blossoms forever in the heart.

Embracing Tender Moments

In the soft light of the dawn,
We awaken to a bond drawn.
Each moment shared, a treasured gift,
Embracing tender moments, hearts uplift.

With every whisper, hopes ignite,
Wrapped in warmth, we hold on tight.
In your gaze, a world so bright,
Embracing love, our guiding light.

Through laughter sweet and tears we share,
In every challenge, we will care.
With gentle hands, we face the storm,
Embracing tender moments, hearts warm.

In silence shared, our spirits meet,
In every heartbeat, love's heartbeat.
With every breath, our souls take flight,
Embracing moments, pure delight.

Let's dance beneath the moonlit skies,
In each other's arms, where comfort lies.
In every glance, a promise made,
Embracing tender moments, never fade.

The Garden of Us

In this garden, love will grow,
With tender care, our hearts will sow.
Each flower blooms through sun and rain,
The garden of us will never wane.

Paths entwined beneath the trees,
Whispers dance upon the breeze.
Hand in hand, we walk as one,
The garden of us, where dreams are spun.

Colors vibrant, scents divine,
Each petal speaks of love, your hand in mine.
In every season, life unfolds,
The garden of us, a story told.

Let the wildflowers freely sway,
In this oasis where we play.
Every moment, cherished and true,
The garden of us, just me and you.

With roots intertwined, we will stand,
In this sacred space, love is grand.
Together we'll weather life's fuss,
In our hearts, the garden of us.

Everlasting Echoes

In the silence of the night,
Whispers dance on soft winds,
Memories linger, softly bright,
Time remembers, love transcends.

Underneath the starlit sky,
Promises etched in the air,
In dreams where shadows lie,
Always a bond we will share.

Voices call from far away,
Echoes of what used to be,
In our hearts, they gently stay,
A timeless, sweet reverie.

With every dawn, a new chance,
To write a story anew,
In the rhythm, we shall dance,
Everlasting, pure and true.

Through the years, we remain,
Hearts entwined in gentle song,
In every smile, in each pain,
Our echoes will carry on.

Bonds Beyond Measure

Like roots that twist in the deep,
Unseen but holding us strong,
In every moment we keep,
In each other, we belong.

Through storms that challenge the soul,
Together, we rise and fall,
Hand in hand, we are whole,
A love that conquers all.

With laughter that fills the air,
And tears that cleanse the heart,
In the whispers that we share,
We're never truly apart.

Each challenge we face is light,
For together, we are bold,
In the warmth of love's pure light,
Our story will be told.

As time weaves its endless thread,
Our bond remains, ever wide,
In each word that goes unsaid,
You are always by my side.

The Melody of Us

In the harmony of our hearts,
A symphony softly plays,
Every note a work of art,
In love's embrace, we stay.

With laughter ringing so clear,
And whispers that soothe the pain,
In every moment, you're near,
Our melody will remain.

The rhythm of life's sweet dance,
Each step a cherished delight,
In your eyes, I find my chance,
To soar like birds in flight.

Together, we'll write our song,
With verses of dreams and hope,
In the chorus where we belong,
Together, we learn to cope.

Through the trials that may come,
In harmony, we'll stand tall,
With you, I'm never alone,
In love, we'll rise above all.

Sheltering Hearts

In a world that feels so cold,
Your love is my warm embrace,
A sanctuary to hold,
In your heart, I've found my place.

Beneath the storms that may rage,
We stand united, so strong,
Through every unwritten page,
In love, we always belong.

With laughter that lights the dark,
And trust that blooms like the rose,
In your eyes, I find the spark,
A garden where love always grows.

In moments of doubt or fear,
Together, we face what's near,
With whispers that calm the storm,
In shelter, our hearts stay warm.

As seasons shift and time flows,
Our bond will not fade away,
In you, my shelter, I chose,
To love you more each day.

Seeds of Affection

In the soil of trust we plant,
Tiny seeds, with gentle chant.
Watered by laughter, love grows tall,
Rooted deep, never to fall.

Sunshine and raindrops, they entwine,
Nurturing petals, so divine.
With every heartbeat, the flowers bloom,
In the garden where love finds room.

As seasons change, we tend with care,
Pulling the weeds that dare despair.
Hand in hand, through sun and rain,
In the boundless field, we share our gain.

The colors rich, a vibrant spread,
Each hue a word that's left unsaid.
Together we thrive, each day anew,
In the sacred space, where love rings true.

From tiny seeds, a legacy,
Grows into what was meant to be.
In the heart's garden, we stand strong,
Forever in this love's sweet song.

Whispers of Affection

In the stillness, voices low,
Secrets shared where soft winds blow.
With every glance, a heart unspools,
The language of love, written in jewels.

Moonlit nights, the stars align,
Telling tales of you and mine.
With every breath, the world feels right,
In this dance under the moonlight.

Gentle touches, stolen sighs,
Bringing warmth and sweet replies.
In your gaze, a universe vast,
Moments cherished, forever to last.

Echoes linger, soft and sweet,
Carried on the winds we meet.
In this space where whispers dwell,
Each moment tells a sacred spell.

Wrapped in silence, hearts comprised,
Knowing well where love resides.
The whispers guide our souls to roam,
In each other's arms, we find our home.

Embrace of Hearts

In the cradle of your arms,
I find shelter, no alarms.
A safe haven, warm and bright,
Love leads us through the night.

With every heartbeat, a silent vow,
An unbroken bond, here and now.
Where dreams converge and spirits soar,
In this embrace, I crave no more.

Through tempest storms and sunny skies,
In your embrace, my spirit flies.
With every touch, the worlds comply,
In the warmth of love, we rise high.

Gentle whispers, tender grace,
In every hug, we find our place.
Two souls united, never apart,
A timeless dance, the beat of the heart.

In the mosaic of every tear,
In laughter shared, we draw near.
Together we thrive, in every way,
In the embrace of hearts, forever to stay.

The Gentle Garden of Us

In a garden where love tends to grow,
With petals soft, and hearts aglow.
Gentle breezes, a fragrant light,
Each moment shared feels so right.

We wander paths of emerald green,
Discovering joys, both felt and seen.
With every bloom, a memory made,
In the gentle garden, none can fade.

In the rustling leaves, we hear the song,
Of nature's whispers, inviting us along.
Hand in hand, our spirits dance,
In the beauty of love, we take a chance.

Sunrise brings a golden hue,
A canvas bright, a world renewed.
With each sunrise, a promise reigns,
In the gentle garden, love sustains.

As seasons pass, we cherish each day,
In this haven, we choose to stay.
Growing together, side by side,
In the gentle garden, our hearts abide.

Sanctuary of Embrace

In the arms of twilight's glow,
We find solace, soft and slow.
Whispers traced in warm caress,
A sacred space, a sweet recess.

Here, hearts merge in tender grace,
Time stands still in this safe space.
With every breath, a love anew,
In this sanctuary, just we two.

The world fades behind a veil,
As silent prayers begin to sail.
In every heartbeat, we belong,
Our souls entwined in love's sweet song.

Wrapped in warmth, no fear or doubt,
In this embrace, we dance about.
An endless journey, hand in hand,
In our sanctuary, we will stand.

Through storms that try to break our mold,
In this embrace, we'll find our gold.
Together strong, through thick and thin,
In our haven, love shall win.

Whispers in the Quiet

In the hush where shadows play,
Gentle whispers guide the way.
Thoughts like feathers drift and sway,
In the quiet, hearts convey.

Rustling leaves, a soft refrain,
Calling out through sweet terrain.
Every sigh a whispered prayer,
In silence, feelings laid bare.

Moonlit beams on tranquil streams,
Lullabies of hopeful dreams.
A tapestry of softest night,
Weaving love's enduring light.

With each star a story told,
In the silence, we'll be bold.
Finding strength in gentle grace,
In these whispers, love we trace.

Moments shared in quiet glee,
Echo softly, just you and me.
In the still, we hear the heart,
Whispers binding, never part.

The Nourishment of Us

In the garden where we grow,
Every seed a love we sow.
Sunlight kisses, rain's embrace,
Nourishing our sacred place.

Roots entangle, strong and deep,
In this bond, our souls we keep.
Water flows like whispered grace,
In harmony, we find our space.

Harvest moons and morning dew,
Every moment shared is true.
From laughter's bloom to sorrows' shade,
In this life, our dreams are laid.

Together thriving, side by side,
In the journey, love our guide.
Every challenge faced with trust,
Together, we are nourished dust.

With every heartbeat, we will tend,
In this journey, love won't end.
Hand in hand, through thick and thin,
In the nourishment, we begin.

Lanterns in the Dark

When shadows linger, dark and deep,
Our lanterns shine, no fear to keep.
With every flicker, hope ignites,
Guiding us through starless nights.

In the dark, our spirits rise,
Lit by love that never dies.
A gentle glow to light the way,
In every heart, a bright array.

With lanterns held, we find our path,
In unity, we share the math.
Counting stars that pierce the gloom,
Together, we create our bloom.

Though the night may stretch its hand,
In our light, we boldly stand.
Through trials faced and dreams embraced,
Lanterns guide with warmth and grace.

In every shadow that is cast,
We find strength in love steadfast.
With lanterns bright, we'll never part,
For in the dark, you have my heart.

Mosaic of Togetherness

In colors bright, we stand as one,
Each piece a voice, a story spun.
With laughter shared and tears embraced,
Together we rise, no love misplaced.

Through trials faced, we hold the thread,
In unity, our hearts are wed.
We weave our dreams in vibrant hues,
Mosaic made of me and you.

The bond we share is woven tight,
In darkest days, we find the light.
Hand in hand, we dance through strife,
In this grand tapestry of life.

With every stitch, our spirits grow,
A canvas marked by joy and woe.
In every crack, our strength is found,
Together, love's true magic's bound.

So let us paint with all our might,
This mosaic bright, our shared delight.
In every shade, a tale does bloom,
Of togetherness, dispelling gloom.

Our Cupped Hands

With open palms, we catch the rain,
In gentle grace, we ease the pain.
Cupped hands cradle dreams unspoken,
In softness, wounds can be broken.

The warmth we share, like sunlight beams,
Our hands united, weaving dreams.
In silent whispers, hope is born,
Together strong, in every morn.

As seasons change, we stand this ground,
In every heartbeat, love is found.
With loving touch, we nurture all,
In cupped hands, we never fall.

So reach for me, and I'll reach too,
In each embrace, we will renew.
With hands entwined, we face our fate,
Together now, it's never late.

In every hold, a promise lies,
Our cupped hands lift our spirits high.
In unity, our strength expands,
Forever blessed, with cupped hands.

Journeys of Compassion

Through winding paths, our hearts we steer,
In every step, we draw love near.
As compassion lights the darkest night,
We journey on, guided by sight.

Each soul we meet, a story deep,
In shared experiences, love we reap.
With open hearts, we learn and grow,
In unity, our spirits flow.

Hands held high, we rise as one,
In every trial, compassion's begun.
The road ahead may twist and bend,
But with each other, we'll transcend.

Oh, let our voices carry far,
In every conflict, be our star.
With acts of kindness, we shall see,
Our shared humanity set free.

Through journeys vast, we forge our way,
In every heart, our love shall stay.
With open minds, we greet the dawn,
In compassion's glow, we journey on.

The Gentle Caress of Home

In whispered winds, the heart does roam,
A sacred space, the gentle home.
With every wall, a tale to tell,
In love's embrace, we choose to dwell.

The laughter rings through halls of light,
A comfort found in every night.
With every corner, memories reside,
In warmth and peace, our hearts abide.

The gentle caress, like a soft breeze,
In every moment, worries seize.
Around the table, stories flow,
In family ties, our spirits grow.

Through open doors and windows wide,
In every guest, love will abide.
It's here we find our roots, our grace,
In every heartbeat, a snug embrace.

So cherish this, our sacred space,
In life's embrace, we find our place.
The gentle caress of home, we share,
In love's warm glow, forever fair.

Reaching Beyond

In the twilight, dreams take flight,
Stars above, whispers of night.
Hands extended, hearts laid bare,
Together we rise, seeking rare.

Miles stretching, horizons wide,
With trust, we navigate the tide.
Each moment sparkles, brightly shines,
Boundless hope in tangled vines.

Through challenges, we boldly tread,
With courage, we forge ahead.
Onward to where the sky meets sea,
In this journey, you and me.

Bridges built from laughter shared,
In every glance, the world is bared.
Hands together, we explore,
In unity, we yearn for more.

Stories woven, threads entwined,
Futures bright, beautifully designed.
With every step, we find our song,
Reaching beyond, where we belong.

Weaving Our Story

In the tapestry of time, we thread,
Moments captured, words unsaid.
Yarns of laughter, strands of tears,
Together we'll conquer, face our fears.

Each chapter blooms like flowers wild,
In the garden where dreams are filed.
We dance through pages, hand in hand,
Crafting a tale, uniquely planned.

Through the storms, we found our way,
With memories bright, welcoming day.
Every heartbeat, every sigh,
A testament to love's sweet tie.

In quiet nights, we pause to breathe,
While weaving tales, we dream, believe.
In colors vibrant, shades of deep,
Our story's promise, ours to keep.

In every line, our path defined,
With threads of hope and love aligned.
We write anew, each dawn, each dusk,
In the bonds we share, we trust.

Cup of Affection

In delicate porcelain, stories swirl,
Warmth of your smile, soft as a pearl.
A potion brewed from heart to heart,
In the cup of affection, we never part.

Sipping moments, rich with grace,
In the warmth of your sweet embrace.
With every drop, we share a dream,
In serene silence, love's gentle steam.

Every sunset served with care,
A taste of peace, sweet and rare.
Laughter sprinkled, like sugar bliss,
In our chalice, a stolen kiss.

Through seasons shifting, time flows free,
In this cup, there's you and me.
Together we find solace and peace,
In every sip, our joys increase.

The brew ignites our passions bright,
Whispers linger in the night.
With every clink, our spirits rise,
In this cup, love never dies.

Reflections in the Stillness

In the quiet where echoes play,
Thoughts unravel, drift away.
Stillness wraps like a gentle shawl,
In this space, we hear the call.

Mirroring souls in tranquil streams,
Fragments dance in softest dreams.
Within the calm, our truths are found,
Where silence sings and hearts resound.

Crisp air holds the secrets deep,
Where shadows linger, softly sleep.
In golden rays, we find our way,
Guided by warmth of light each day.

Moments echo, softly flow,
In reflection, we learn and grow.
Beneath the stars, our worries cease,
In the stillness, we find sweet peace.

With every breath, we pause to feel,
The beauty that life can reveal.
Through gentle whispers, we connect,
In reflections, love's true effect.

Milestones of Connection

In quiet whispers, hands entwined,
We trace the steps of our own design.
Each laugh a stone, each tear a thread,
Building bridges where once we tread.

Through seasons shifting, side by side,
In shared adventures, we take pride.
Moments captured, a timeless dance,
In fragile ties, we find our chance.

The road is long, yet we remain,
With hearts ablaze, we greet the rain.
Together we face both night and dawn,
With every heartbeat, we carry on.

Though storms may roar and shadows loom,
In unity, we find our room.
With every turn, we redefine,
The essence of our grand design.

In every story, a love embedded,
In the book of life, our tales are threaded.
Through milestones vast, our spirits soar,
In every moment, we seek for more.

Petals of Shared Memories

Fleeting moments, like petals fall,
Each one cherished, a fragrant call.
In gardens lush, we planted dreams,
Where laughter bloomed and sunlight beams.

Seasons change, yet roots run deep,
In every memory, love we keep.
With every dance, the past unveiled,
In silent echoes, our hearts exhaled.

With every smile, a story spun,
In the tapestry, we are one.
Through trials faced, we found a way,
In shared memories, we long to stay.

Time may weather, yet still we hold,
The petals captured, the moments bold.
In fragile beauty, together we stand,
Crafting memories, hand in hand.

A bouquet vibrant, our lives entwined,
In every petal, love defined.
Through every breath, the past remains,
In petals of shared memories, our love sustains.

Radiance of Belonging

In warm embraces, spirits glow,
Where hearts ignite, and friendships grow.
In laughter's light, we find our place,
In every smile, a warm embrace.

Through trials faced, we lift each other,
In unity, we find a mother.
With every hug, the world feels right,
In shared dreams, we share our light.

A circle formed, both strong and wide,
In the radiance, we take pride.
Hand in hand, we reach for stars,
In belonging's warmth, we heal our scars.

Through whispered secrets and joyful noise,
We celebrate our shared joys.
In the simplest moments, bond is true,
In the radiance of belonging, I see you.

Each heartbeat echoes, a rhythmic sound,
In this haven, love is found.
With every story, we come alive,
In the radiance, together we thrive.

Harmonious Echoes

In the stillness, we can hear,
The echoes of love, crystal clear.
With every note, our hearts align,
In harmonious rhythms, we intertwine.

Through laughter's song, and whispers soft,
In melodies sweet, our spirits lift.
In every chord, a tale is spun,
In harmonious echoes, we become one.

Together we dance to life's refrain,
In harmony, we bear the strain.
With each experience, we learn and grow,
In shared echoes, our souls aglow.

Across the mountains, and through the trees,
Our symphony flows with the breeze.
In every heartbeat, our love resounds,
In harmonious echoes, joy abounds.

Through storms that rage and skies that gray,
In united voices, we find our way.
A chorus of hearts, forever free,
In harmonious echoes, you and me.

Soft Echoes of Attachment

In whispers soft, your voice calls near,
A gentle nudge, a feeling clear.
Each heartbeat's pulse, a soothing song,
In quiet moments, where we belong.

Threads of memory, woven tight,
Beneath the stars, in the pale moonlight.
Every glance shared, a spark of fire,
Fueling the depths of our desire.

The rustling leaves, the breeze that sighs,
Carry our hopes to the endless skies.
In each soft echo, your love I find,
A timeless bond that fate designed.

With fingers entwined, we chase the dawn,
Two souls as one, forever drawn.
In silence shared, a promise bright,
Our hearts aligned, a guiding light.

Soft whispers dance in the twilight air,
In every moment, I feel you there.
Roots of affection, deep and wide,
In the garden of us, hearts open wide.

Roots of Devotion

Beneath the soil, our roots entwine,
In shared embrace, your heart is mine.
Through seasons change, our love will grow,
In every trial, our strength will show.

With every dawn, a brand new start,
In whispers sweet, you own my heart.
The storms may rage, the winds may howl,
But here we stand, steady as aowl.

Branches stretch toward the sky so blue,
With every breath, I'm drawn to you.
Our dreams like leaves, in vibrant hues,
In endless skies, we'll chase our truths.

With roots so deep, we'll weather time,
In every moment, our spirits climb.
Together, we'll forge a path unknown,
In the garden of love, forever grown.

From humble seeds, a forest stands,
In unity's grasp, we join our hands.
Our roots of devotion, strong and true,
In every heartbeat, I'll cherish you.

The Symphony of Us

In harmony, our hearts compose,
A melody that gently flows.
Each laugh, a note; each sigh, a chord,
Together, the music we've adored.

With rhythms shared, we dance each day,
In syncopation, we find our way.
The highs and lows, a perfect tune,
In twilight's glow, beneath the moon.

Like waves that crash on distant shores,
Our love crescendos, forever soars.
In every heartbeat, a vibrant sound,
In the symphony of us, we are bound.

The world around fades into silence,
In your embrace, I find my balance.
Our music whispers through the night,
A serenade, our souls unite.

As melodies blend and intertwine,
In chords of love, we redefine.
In every note, my heart will remain,
In the symphony of us, eternal refrain.

Lanterns in the Dark

In shadows cast, where silence lies,
Your love, a lantern, in darkened skies.
It guides me through the deepest night,
Illuminating all that's right.

With flickering flames, our hopes ignite,
Each whispered dream becomes a light.
Together we shine, a beacon bright,
In the darkest places, we unite.

As storms may rage and tempests blow,
Your steady flame will always show.
A flicker here, a spark of grace,
In every challenge, our hearts embrace.

Like lanterns swaying in the breeze,
Your presence calms, it puts me at ease.
In shadows where the worries dwell,
Your love, a story I long to tell.

So hold my hand, let's face the dark,
As lanterns glow with every spark.
Together we'll light this endless night,
In the warmth of love, forever bright.

A Sanctuary of Caring

In shadows deep, we find the light,
A place where hearts feel safe and bright.
With open arms, we gather near,
Creating bonds that calm the fear.

Whispers of kindness drift through air,
In every gesture, love laid bare.
A tender glance, a gentle nod,
This sanctuary feels like God.

Within these walls, our spirits mend,
In laughter shared, our souls can blend.
With every tear, a story shared,
In this warm space, we feel prepared.

Compassion flows, a river wide,
In hearts united, none can hide.
Together strong, we rise and stand,
In this safe space, we lend a hand.

So here's to love, a sacred thread,
In caring hearts, where hope is fed.
A sanctuary built on trust,
In every moment, love is just.

Love's Gentle Hands

With hands that soothe, hearts intertwine,
In every touch, a spark divine.
Whispers soft, like evening breeze,
In love's embrace, we find our ease.

Each moment shared, a dance so sweet,
In every glance, our souls compete.
Love's gentle hands, a guide so true,
In every heartbeat, I find you.

Through trials faced, we build our trust,
Together strong, we rise from dust.
In love's cocoon, we learn to grow,
With gentle hands, we steal the show.

Every laugh, a melody bright,
In love's embrace, the world feels right.
With open hearts, we brave the day,
In love's gentle hands, we'll find our way.

A tapestry woven, thread by thread,
In every moment, love is spread.
Through all we face, we stand as one,
With love's gentle hands, we have won.

Healing Touch of Togetherness

In silence shared, our spirits rise,
In every hug, a warm surprise.
With loving care, we hold so tight,
A healing touch, our hearts take flight.

Through storms that rage, we find our calm,
In every heartbeat, a soothing balm.
Our laughter echoes, a sweet refrain,
In togetherness, we break the chain.

Through darkest nights, we walk in light,
With hands entwined, we face the fright.
In unity, we find our song,
With healing touch, we all belong.

Every tear, a bond we share,
In every smile, we lay our care.
In moments vast, or small and brief,
Together strong, we master grief.

A network spun from love's embrace,
In every heart, we find our place.
With healing touch, we journey far,
In togetherness, we are the stars.

The Brightness of Affection

In every glance, the warmth ignites,
A gentle spark that feels so right.
Affection shines like morning dew,
In every moment, I see you.

Through laughter bright, we dance with glee,
In every touch, the world we see.
The brightness glows in love's embrace,
With every heartbeat, a tender space.

With every word, a promise made,
In love's garden, our hearts cascade.
Affection blooms in vibrant hues,
In every thought, it softly pursues.

Together we stand, hand in hand,
In this bright light, we'll always land.
Through every trial, our spirits soar,
The brightness of affection, evermore.

With open hearts, we face the dawn,
In love's embrace, we greet each morn.
Together in this radiant glow,
In affection's warmth, we'll always grow.

Embracing the Softness

In the quiet dawn, we find our peace,
Gentle whispers of the morning breeze.
Softly wrapped in warmth of light,
Our hearts awaken, spirits bright.

Cocooned in moments, tender and true,
Each heartbeat echoes, a love anew.
Together we journey, hand in hand,
In every touch, we understand.

The petals fall with grace so fine,
A tapestry woven, yours and mine.
With every sigh, the world feels light,
In the soft embrace, we find our flight.

Through the valleys low, and mountains high,
Our laughter dances across the sky.
In shadows cast, we still find glow,
In softness, we flourish, love will grow.

Life's gentle rhythm, we sway along,
In the hush of night, we sing our song.
Embracing softness, our spirits soar,
In unity's cradle, forevermore.

Pathways of Companionship

Two souls walking on a winding path,
Echoes of laughter, love's sweet aftermath.
Side by side, we face each day,
In every step, we find our way.

Moments crafted, memories sown,
In shared glances, we have grown.
Hands entwined, we move as one,
In sunlight's glow, our lives begun.

The trees whisper secrets, stories unfold,
In pathways of companionship, we are bold.
Through storms we gather, our spirits strong,
In silence and chatter, we both belong.

With every mile, the bond does deepen,
Through shadows and light, our hearts do beacon.
In tender moments, we learn to see,
Together we flourish, you and me.

The beauty of journey, forever embraced,
In laughter and tears, our fear is faced.
With each new dawn, a gift that's true,
Pathways of companionship, me and you.

The Dance of Togetherness

Under the moon's soft silver glow,
We twirl and sway, lost in the flow.
In the rhythm of life, we find our tune,
Dancing together, night and noon.

With every step, our hearts take flight,
In synchrony, we ignite the night.
Whispers of joy, the world fades away,
In the dance of togetherness, we play.

The music swells, our spirits rise,
In the embrace of love, we realize.
With open arms, we welcome grace,
In every moment, we find our place.

A waltz of dreams, a ballet of trust,
In each gentle turn, our love is robust.
We glide through the air, time slips past,
In the dance of togetherness, we last.

With the dawn's light, we slow our pace,
Yet the melody lingers, leaving a trace.
In every heartbeat, our souls entwined,
The dance of togetherness, beautifully designed.

Blooming in Our Presence

In the garden of time, we plant our dreams,
Where love blossoms in silver streams.
With every seedling, hope takes root,
Blooming in our presence, wild and true.

Sunlight dances on petals bright,
Each moment cherished, a pure delight.
With laughter's echo, flowers unfold,
In our hearts, the stories told.

Together we nurture, tend with care,
In the soil of trust, our love lays bare.
Through seasons changing, we stand strong,
Blooming in our presence, where we belong.

With gentle rains, we wash away fears,
In the fabric of life, we thread our years.
Each bloom represents a promise made,
In vibrant colors, never to fade.

As petals unfurl, our souls entwine,
In the lush embrace, your hand in mine.
With every sunrise, new blossoms appear,
Blooming in our presence, forever near.

Echoes of Endearment

In whispers soft, where shadows play,
Love's tender glances light the way.
A heartfelt laugh, a gentle sigh,
Together we'll reach for the sky.

Memories dance like autumn leaves,
In every note, our spirit weaves.
A bond unbroken, never worn,
In silent moments, we are reborn.

Time stands still in your embrace,
Each heartbeat murmurs, love's sweet grace.
Through trials faced, we'll stand as one,
In the warmth of us, we find the sun.

Echoes linger, soft and mild,
In every tear, a joy compiled.
We nurture dreams, like flowers bloom,
Creating light within the gloom.

So let the world around us swirl,
For in your arms, I find my pearl.
A treasure deep, with roots entwined,
In echoes sweet, our love defined.

The Tapestry of Together

Each thread we weave, a story told,
In vibrant hues of blue and gold.
Hand in hand, we shape our fate,
In every moment, love creates.

Time threads through our cherished days,
In laughter's echo and gentle rays.
The fabric thickens, rich and strong,
In shared heartbeats, we belong.

From quiet nights to morning's glow,
Through every ebb, through every flow.
Together, we chart the open sea,
In the tapestry of you and me.

With every dream that lights the way,
We find our strength in what we say.
Bound by love, through dark and light,
Our woven hearts take endless flight.

In every stitch, a promise blooms,
In every laugh, a joy that looms.
Together stitched, never apart,
The tapestry of love, our art.

Seasons of Companionship

In spring's embrace, we start anew,
With vibrant blooms and skies so blue.
Together we laugh, we dance in rain,
Through every joy, through every pain.

Summer's glow brings warmth and light,
With every day, our hearts take flight.
We stroll in fields of golden grain,
Sharing secrets, love's sweet gain.

As autumn leaves begin to fall,
We gather memories, one and all.
In cozy nights, and fireside tales,
Our love endures, through winds and gales.

Winter's chill may cover the land,
But in your heart, I find my stand.
Wrapped in blankets, close we stay,
In the warmth of us, we'll find the way.

Through every season, hand in hand,
In every moment, we understand.
For in companionship, we find our home,
No matter where, no need to roam.

The Embrace of Souls

In stillness found, our spirits meet,
Two worlds collide, in harmony sweet.
A silent pact, in gazes locked,
In every heartbeat, time is blocked.

With open arms, our fears release,
In tender moments, we find our peace.
Beneath the stars, we share our dreams,
In the night's silence, love redeems.

Through trials faced, we rise as one,
In every struggle, battles won.
A bond transcending all that's seen,
In the embrace of souls, our sheen.

Together we weather the fiercest storm,
In chaos bright, we find our form.
In whispered vows and gentle grace,
Our souls entwine, a sacred space.

So let the world around us spin,
For in this love, we've truly won.
In every heartbeat, every fold,
The embrace of souls, a story told.

Tending to Our Garden

In the early light we meet,
With hands in soil, hearts complete.
We nurture dreams with gentle care,
Together, we find beauty rare.

The weeds of doubt we cast away,
In our garden, hope holds sway.
Each flower blooms, a tale to tell,
In this haven where we dwell.

The sun will rise, the rain will fall,
In every season, we stand tall.
With patience, love, and tender touch,
Our garden grows, we cherish much.

Through storms that rage and winds that blow,
Our roots entwined, we'll always grow.
In every petal, color bright,
We find our joy, our shared delight.

As twilight falls, we pause to see,
The fruits of love, our legacy.
In every seed, a promise sown,
In this garden, we've made our home.

Seeds of Devotion

In every heart, a seed is sown,
With whispered hopes, it finds a home.
Through trials faced, we tend the ground,
In love's embrace, new strength is found.

With sunlight's grace, we stand so tall,
Each moment shared, we heed the call.
As roots grow deep, we learn to trust,
In bonds of loyalty, endless just.

The winds may shift, the rains may pour,
Yet our foundation, strong at the core.
Each season's change, a chance to start,
For every seed, we plant our heart.

In gardens vast, with blooms so bright,
We find our way, through day and night.
In every petal, a soft refrain,
Of moments cherished, of joy and pain.

So let us nurture, with gentle hands,
The seeds of love, in all our plans.
Together we'll grow, through thick and thin,
In the garden of life, let us begin.

Blossoms in the Moonlight

Underneath the silver moon,
Soft petals dance, a gentle tune.
In twilight's glow, our dreams take flight,
Together lost in the magic of night.

The fragrant air, a sweet embrace,
Under the stars, we find our place.
With whispered words, we touch the sky,
In the shadowed light, we learn to fly.

The garden sleeps, but love awakes,
In every breath, a new path breaks.
With laughter shared under the stars,
We chase our hopes, forget the scars.

As dawn approaches, colors blend,
In every moment, love transcends.
With every blossom, our spirits rise,
In this moonlit dance, we find our prize.

So let us linger, hold on tight,
Beneath the glow of soft moonlight.
In the hush of night, our souls unite,
In this tender garden, hearts ignite.

Cultivating Togetherness

With every step, we walk as one,
In fields of green, our journey's begun.
Through trials faced, hand in hand,
Side by side, we'll make our stand.

In laughter shared, our spirits soar,
Through ups and downs, we seek for more.
Each seed we plant, a dream expressed,
In this life together, we are blessed.

The path may twist, the road may bend,
Yet together we rise, through each trend.
In the joy of growth, we find our way,
Through sunshine bright and somber gray.

In shared moments, love will bloom,
Bringing light to every room.
With tender hearts, we cultivate,
This garden of life, our shared fate.

So let us cherish, every day,
In togetherness, we'll always stay.
With roots entwined and visions clear,
In this garden, we flourish here.

The Language of Tenderness

Whispers softly in the night,
Gentle words take graceful flight.
Each glance a warm embrace,
In this sweet, sacred space.

Fingers brush like a soft breeze,
Carrying secrets with such ease.
Silent vows in every gesture,
Moments held, a quiet treasure.

In your eyes, kindness dances bright,
A world of love, pure and light.
Promises linger in the air,
Each heartbeat says, 'I care'.

Beneath the moon, hearts entwine,
In every sigh, the stars align.
Tender moments weave a song,
In this language, we belong.

Together we speak, soft and true,
In every touch, a world anew.
Creating stories, deep and vast,
A gentle future, bright and cast.

Echoes of Commitment

In every promise, a beacon bright,
A firm resolve, our hearts in sight.
Through trials faced, hand in hand,
In our unity, we firmly stand.

Words we've spoken, strong and clear,
A bond unbroken, we hold dear.
With every challenge that we face,
Love's echo fills this sacred space.

Time may bring its wear and tear,
Yet in your eyes, I find my prayer.
With every heartbeat, I renew
This vow of love, forever true.

Moments shared, each one a thread,
Woven tightly, love widespread.
In laughter's echo, in silence too,
Commitment whispers, 'I love you'.

Together we build, never apart,
A house of dreams, a work of art.
In echoes of our shared delight,
We'll find our way, through day and night.

Caress of Reassurance

In shadows deep, your hand finds mine,
A touch that says, 'You will be fine'.
With gentle care, you mend my fears,
Your presence calms, like soothing tears.

In whispered tones, you wrap me tight,
With every word, you bring the light.
Through stormy seas, your faith stands strong,
In your embrace, I find my song.

Each reassuring glance we share,
A promise made, so pure and rare.
In softest breaths, our worries fade,
In love's embrace, we're unafraid.

The world can spin, but we remain,
A shelter found through joy and pain.
In every heartbeat, your love flows,
A river deep, where safety grows.

With you beside me, skies stay clear,
Each gentle caress, a way to steer.
Together, we'll face the unknown,
In this journey, we're never alone.

Love Under the Stars

Beneath the heavens, our dreams collide,
In the cosmos, we take our ride.
Starlit whispers fill the night,
Our hearts ablaze, a dazzling light.

With every twinkle, secrets laid,
In tender gazes, futures made.
A universe of hopes unfurled,
Love's constellation, our shared world.

Hand in hand, we trace the sky,
Mapping moments as time slips by.
Each shooting star, a wish in flight,
Together, we chase the endless night.

In silence shared, our spirits dance,
Magic woven in every glance.
The moon looks down, a watchful guide,
In this embrace, we coincide.

So let the world fade into dreams,
For under stars, love truly beams.
With every heartbeat, strong yet far,
We find forever, 'neath the stars.

Shaping Our Affection

In whispered words, our hearts entwine,
Two souls converge, a dance divine.
With every glance, our spirits soar,
Together we bloom, forevermore.

The warmth we share ignites the night,
In tender dreams, we find our light.
Each touch a brush, on canvas bare,
Artistry crafted in love's own care.

Through storms we stand, unbreakable,
Building our world, unmistakable.
In laughter's echo, in sorrow's tear,
We shape our bond, year after year.

Two hearts beat as one, a symphony,
Melodies played in harmony.
With patience sown, our roots grow deep,
In quiet moments, our secrets keep.

Together we venture, hand in hand,
Mapping the stars, a dreamland planned.
In every breath, our journey's grace,
Shaping affection, an endless embrace.

Love's Bountiful Harvest

In early sun, we plant our seeds,
With tender care, fulfilling needs.
Through seasons' change, our roots expand,
Love's bountiful harvest, hand in hand.

As blossoms bloom, we reap the joy,
A treasure trove, no one can destroy.
In laughter's rain, and trials' dust,
We gather strength, in love we trust.

Every fruit we share, sweet and ripe,
Nourishing souls, a vibrant type.
In fields of dreams, we wander free,
Love's harvest time, just you and me.

With open hearts, we farm our fate,
Turn moments into joys innate.
Together we stand, steadfast and true,
In every dawn, love's promise renews.

Through winter's chill and summer's glow,
Our bonds deepen, steadily grow.
With every step, we forge our path,
Love's bountiful harvest, a shared aftermath.

The Comfort of Consistency

In morning light, your hand in mine,
Moments flow like aged wine.
Routine embraces, the familiar fold,
In gentle warmth, love's stories told.

Each coffee shared, each laugh's delight,
Grounded in trust, morning to night.
The little things, a soothing balm,
In the chaos, you keep me calm.

Through mundane days, we weave our thread,
In constant whispers, softly said.
A tether strong, against the storm,
In every hug, we feel the warm.

Your smile's the anchor in my sea,
A beacon bright, just you and me.
With every glance, a promise made,
In the comfort of love, our fears allayed.

In quiet evenings, we find our peace,
In every ritual, our joys release.
Together we stand, in life's ballet,
The comfort of consistency, come what may.

Together in Every Breath

In silence shared, our spirits dance,
A union formed, a fateful chance.
With every heartbeat, time stands still,
Together we rise, through sheer will.

In the gentle sighs, we find our song,
Two souls merged, where we belong.
The world fades out, just you and I,
Together we soar, we touch the sky.

In whispers soft, our dreams take flight,
Guided by the stars, through the night.
Every heartbeat, a promise true,
Together in breath, I'm lost in you.

Through life's journey, hand in hand,
Together we navigate, understand.
In all that we share, love's essence flows,
Together in every breath, it grows.

In laughter and tears, we find our way,
Writing our tale, come what may.
With every moment, love's tapestry weaves,
Together in every breath, our hearts believe.

Harvesting Joy Together

In fields of gold, we sow our dreams,
Each moment shared, a sunbeam's gleam.
With laughter's echo, we gather near,
Harvesting joy, spreading good cheer.

Each hand in hand, we toil and sweat,
Creating memories, we won't forget.
In the warmth of the season, hearts unite,
Harvesting joy, our souls take flight.

Sunrise to sunset, we plant with care,
Life's bountiful gifts, a treasure rare.
Through every challenge, we stand strong,
Together we thrive, where we belong.

A tapestry woven with love and grace,
Each thread a story, a warm embrace.
With hopeful hearts, we reap our prize,
In the garden of life, our spirits rise.

As seasons change, our bond remains,
Through joy and sorrow, through losses and gains.
In this dance of life, we find our way,
Harvesting joy together, day by day.

Hearts in Bloom

In the springtime sun, our spirits soar,
Hearts in bloom, forevermore.
With petals bright, we paint the air,
In every smile, love's beauty rare.

The fragrance sweet, a gentle sigh,
In gardens lush, our dreams comply.
With hands entwined, we face the day,
Hearts in bloom, in a dance we play.

Through rain and storm, we stand as one,
Under the clouds, we find the sun.
With every challenge, we start anew,
In this vibrant world, my heart sees you.

In whispers soft, our hopes take flight,
With every heartbeat, we'll chase the light.
Together we'll grow, as the seasons turn,
Hearts in bloom, for love we yearn.

As time goes on, our garden thrives,
With every memory, our love arrives.
In this beautiful life, we'll always find,
Hearts in bloom, forever intertwined.

The Glow of Togetherness

Under the stars, our laughter glows,
In the warmth of togetherness, love grows.
With joyous hearts, we light the night,
In every shadow, shines our light.

In every moment shared, time stands still,
With every heartbeat, our dreams fulfill.
Hand in hand, through thick and thin,
In this glow of love, we always win.

Through every trial, we find our way,
In the glow of togetherness, come what may.
With open hearts, we chase the dawn,
In this sacred bond, we carry on.

In silence shared, a touch so sweet,
In this glow of love, we find our beat.
With every smile, a spark ignites,
Together we shine, through darkest nights.

As seasons change, our fire burns bright,
With love as our guide, we take flight.
In the glow of togetherness, we'll forever roam,
Hand in hand, with hearts as home.

Cherished Embraces

In the warmth of your arms, I find my peace,
Cherished embraces, worries cease.
With every hug, a story told,
In gentle whispers, love unfolds.

In the dance of time, we sway as one,
Every heartbeat, a melody spun.
Through trials faced, we rise above,
In cherished embraces, we find our love.

With laughter shared, we paint the sky,
In every moment, love will fly.
Through stormy weather, we hold on tight,
In cherished embraces, everything feels right.

With each soft glance, our spirits soar,
In endless hugs, we always want more.
Together we stand, through thick and thin,
In cherished embraces, our journey begins.

As years unfurl, our bond will grow,
In these warm moments, love's gentle glow.
Forever wrapped in love's sweet grace,
In cherished embraces, we find our place.

Milton Keynes UK
Ingram Content Group UK Ltd.
UKHW020706021124
450515UK00005B/22